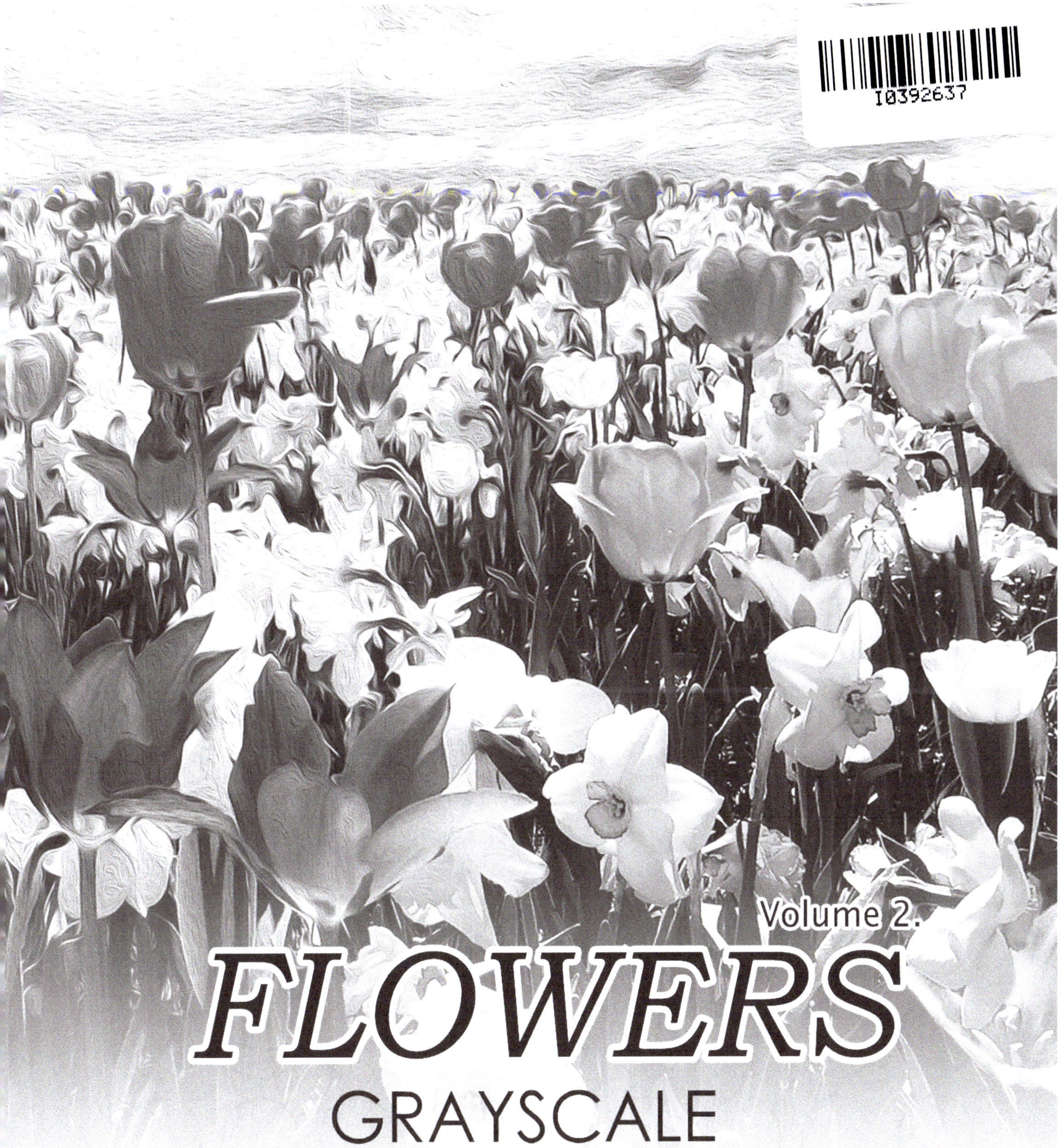

Volume 2.

FLOWERS

GRAYSCALE LANDSCAPE

COLORING BOOKS

COLOR TEST PAGE

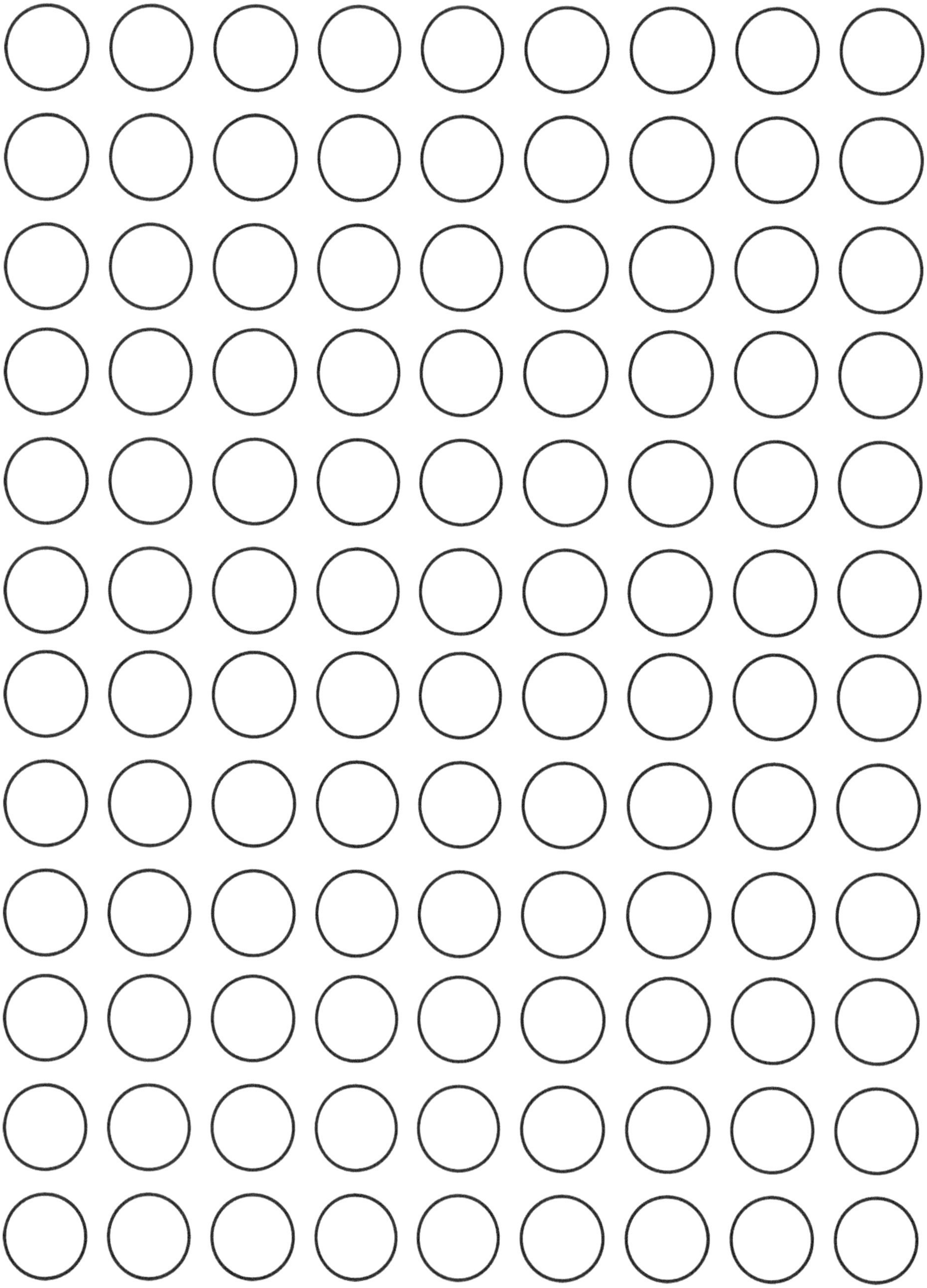

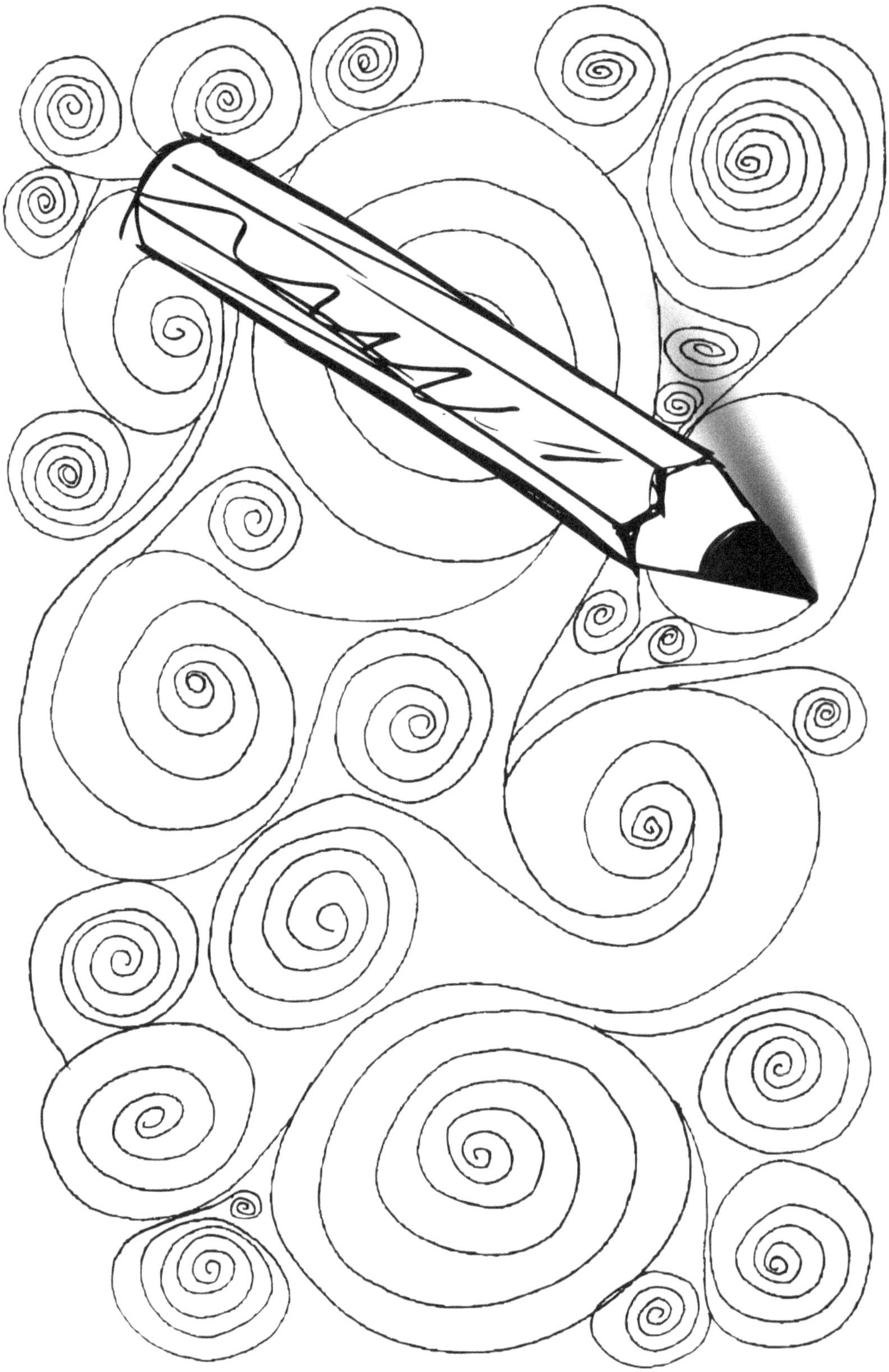

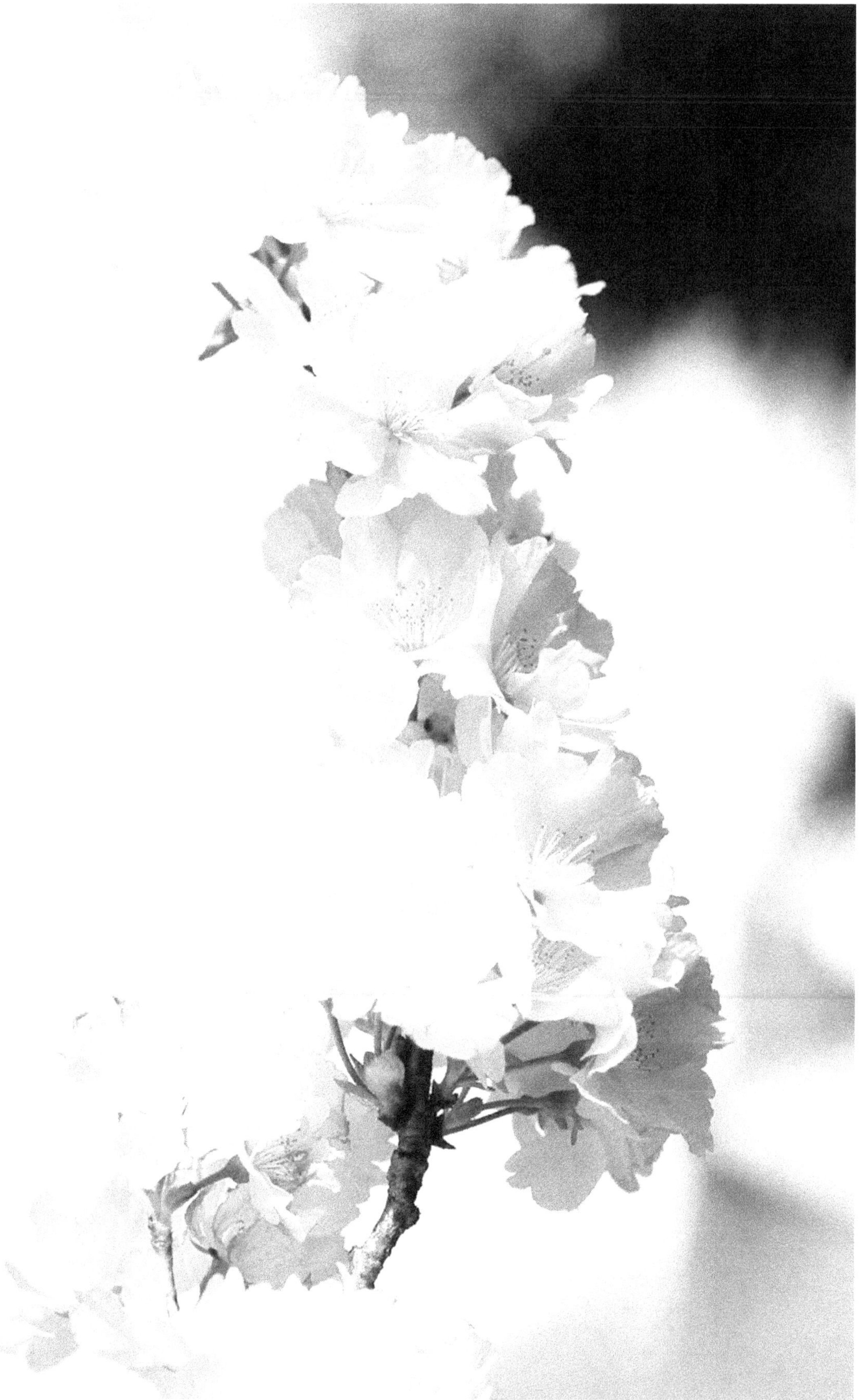

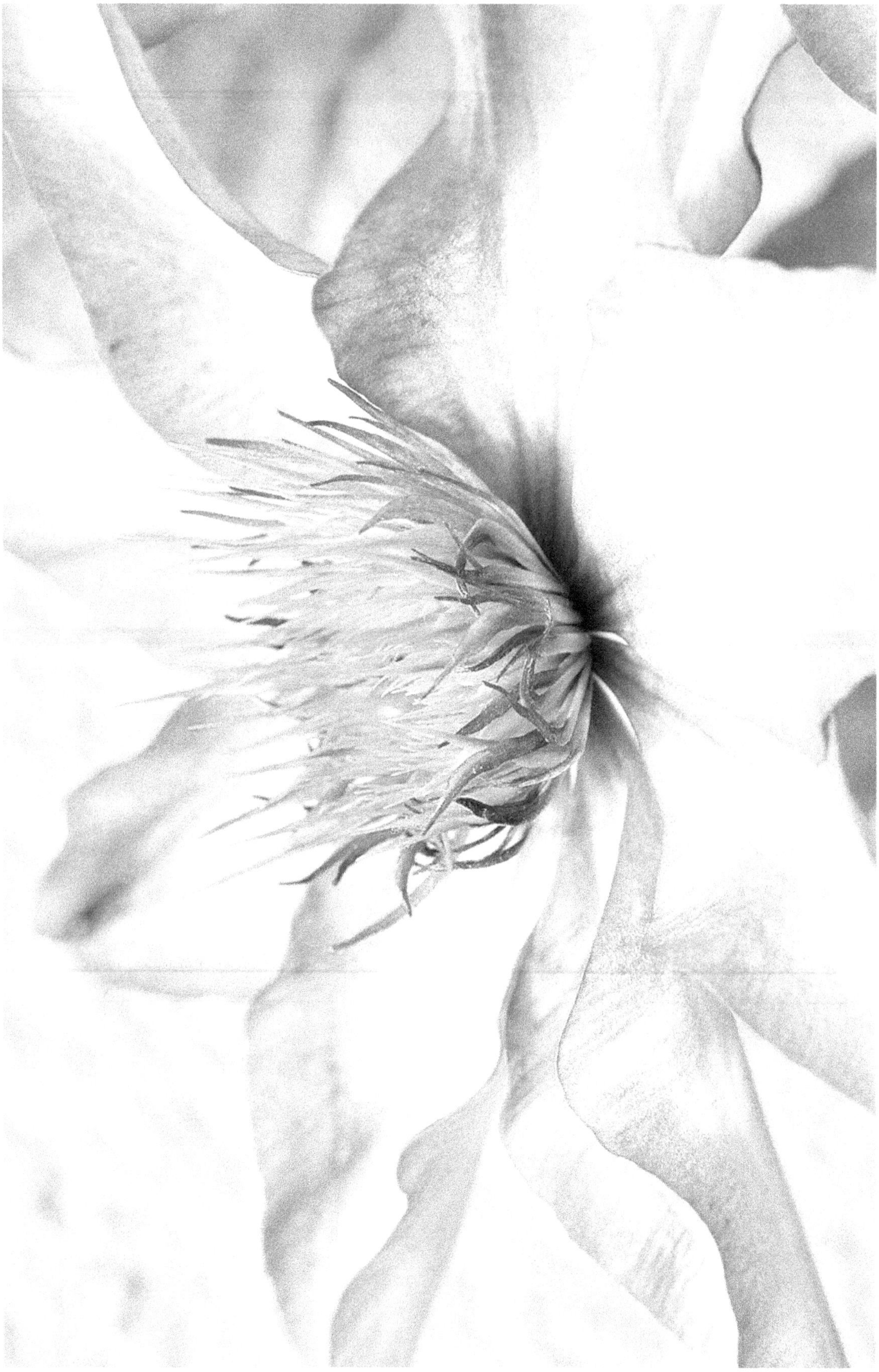

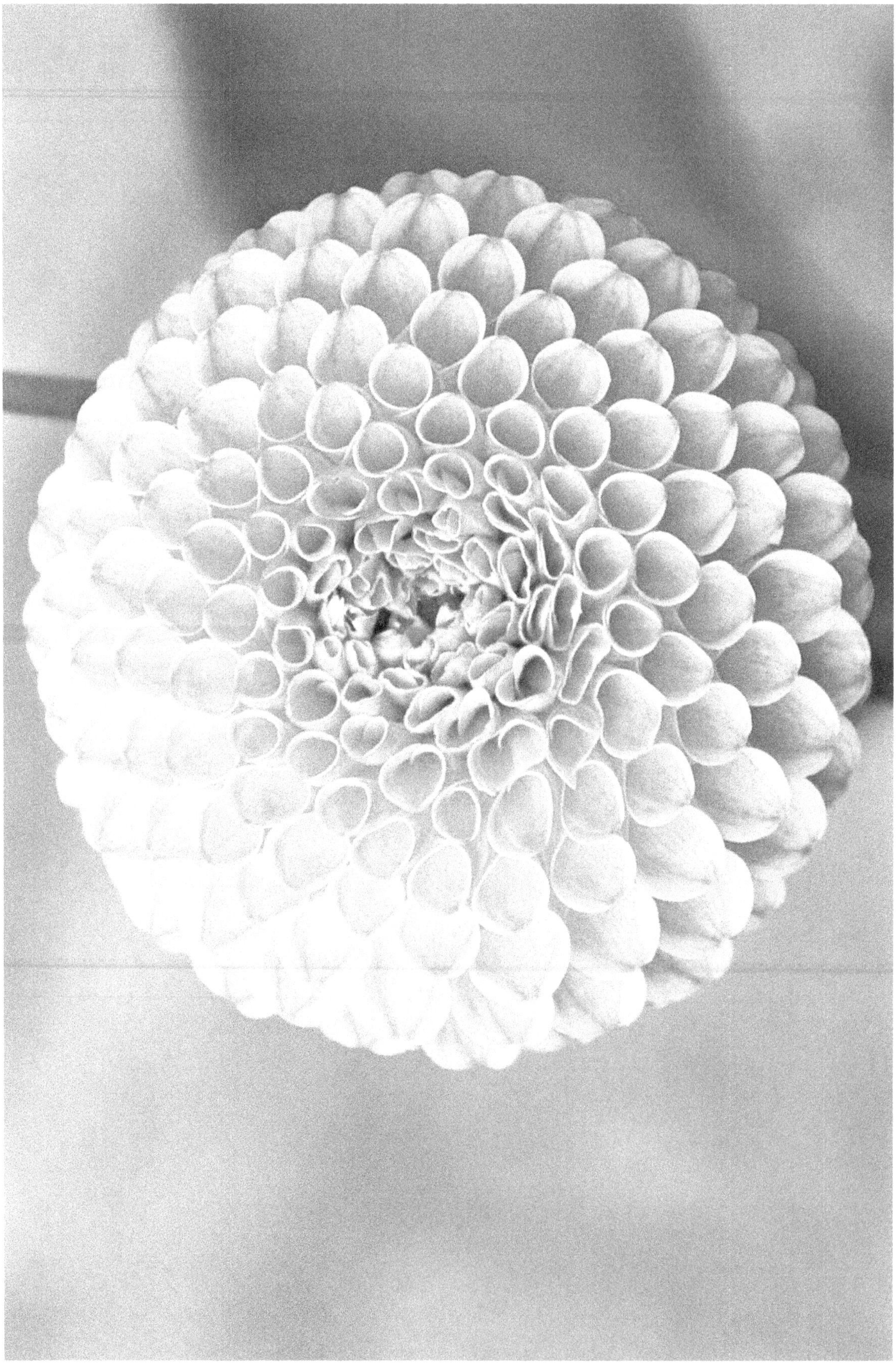

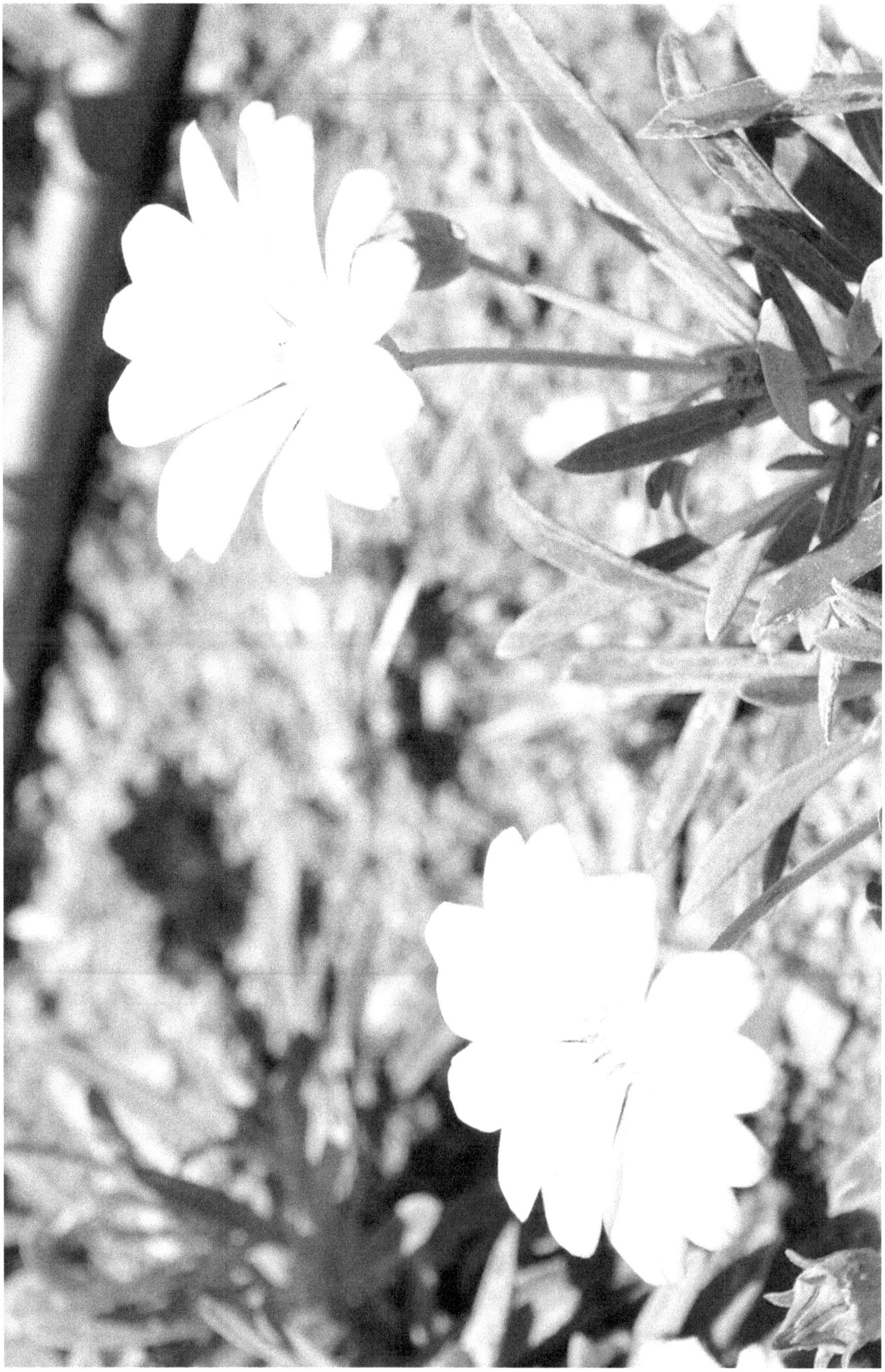

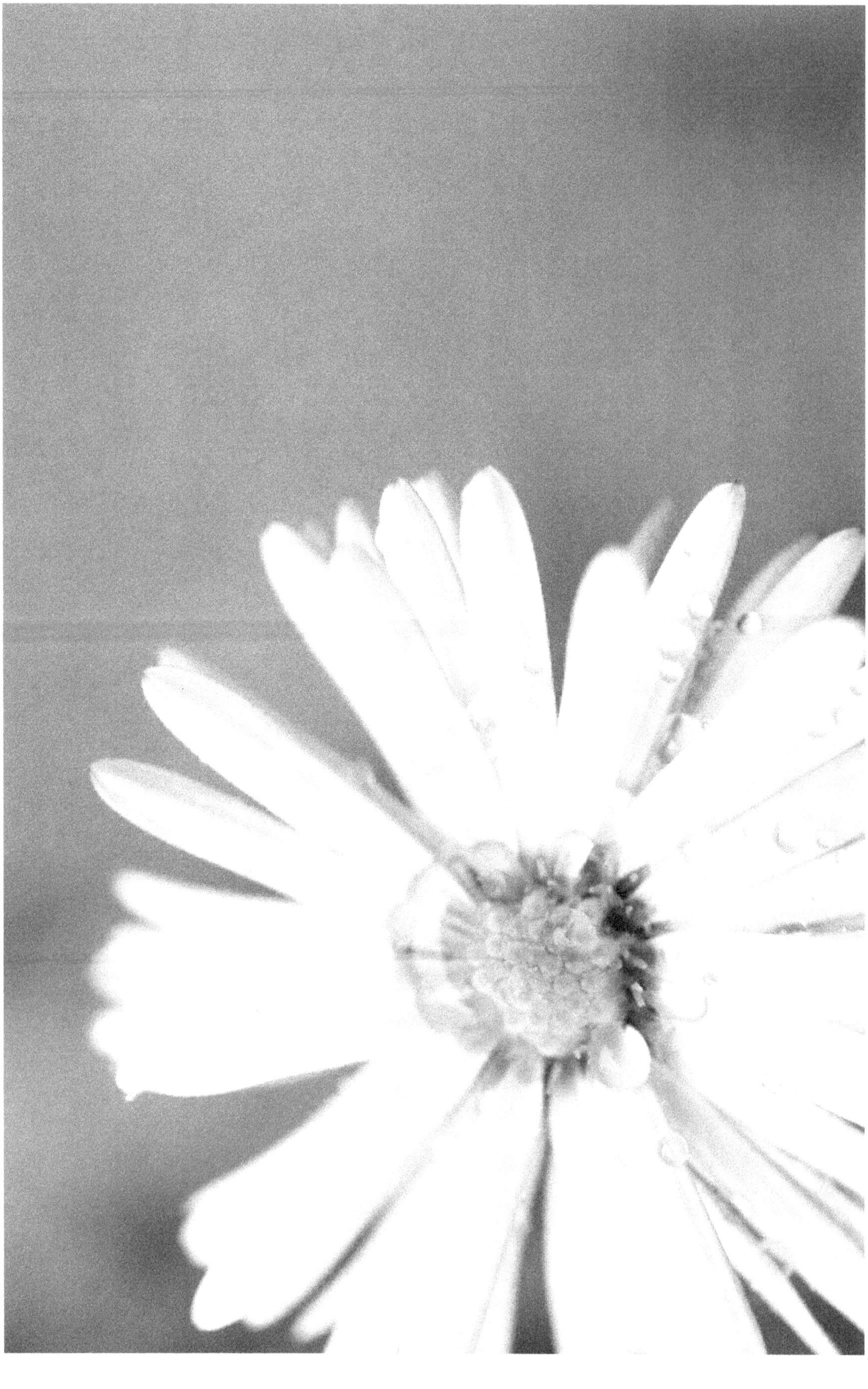

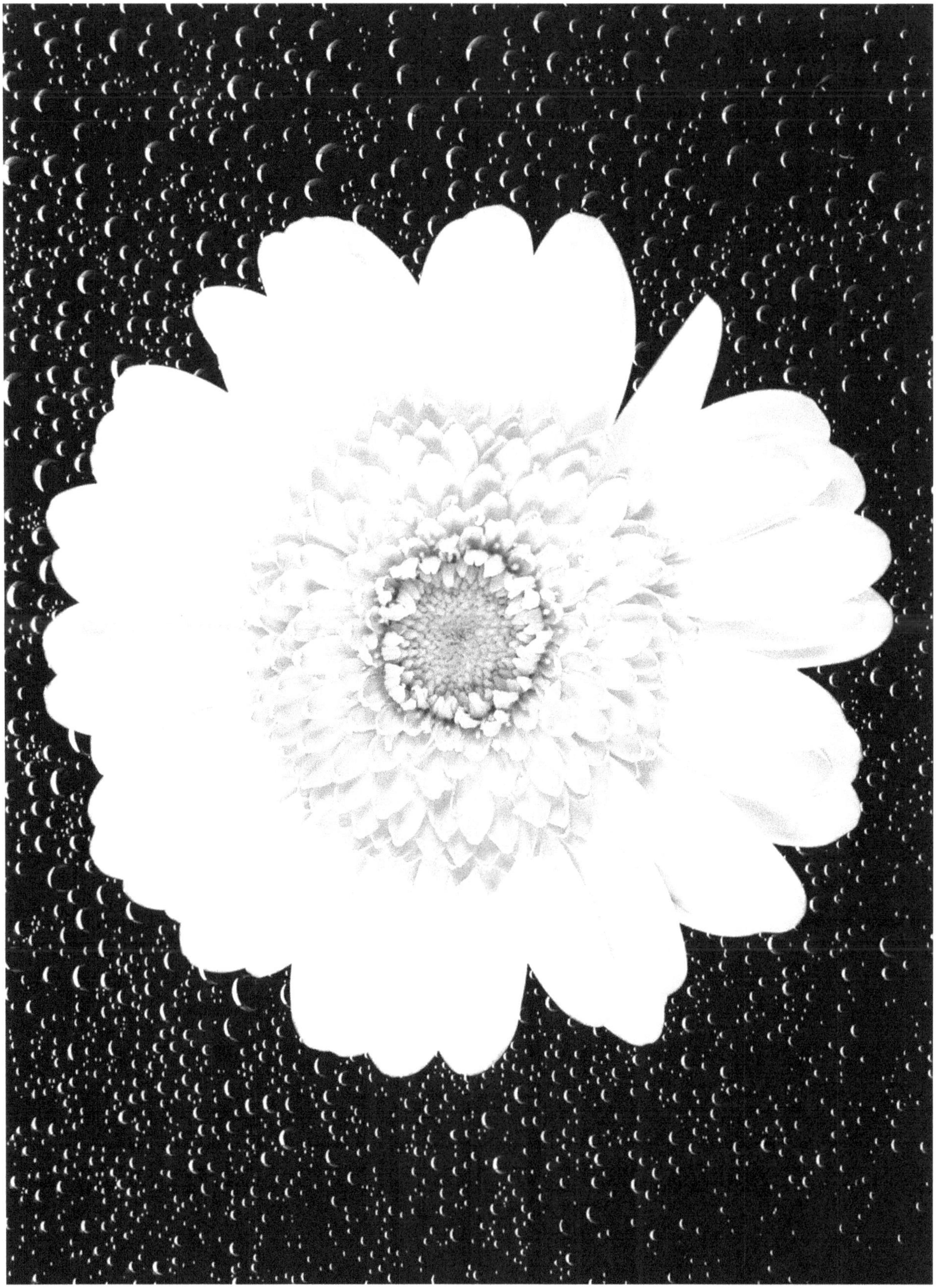

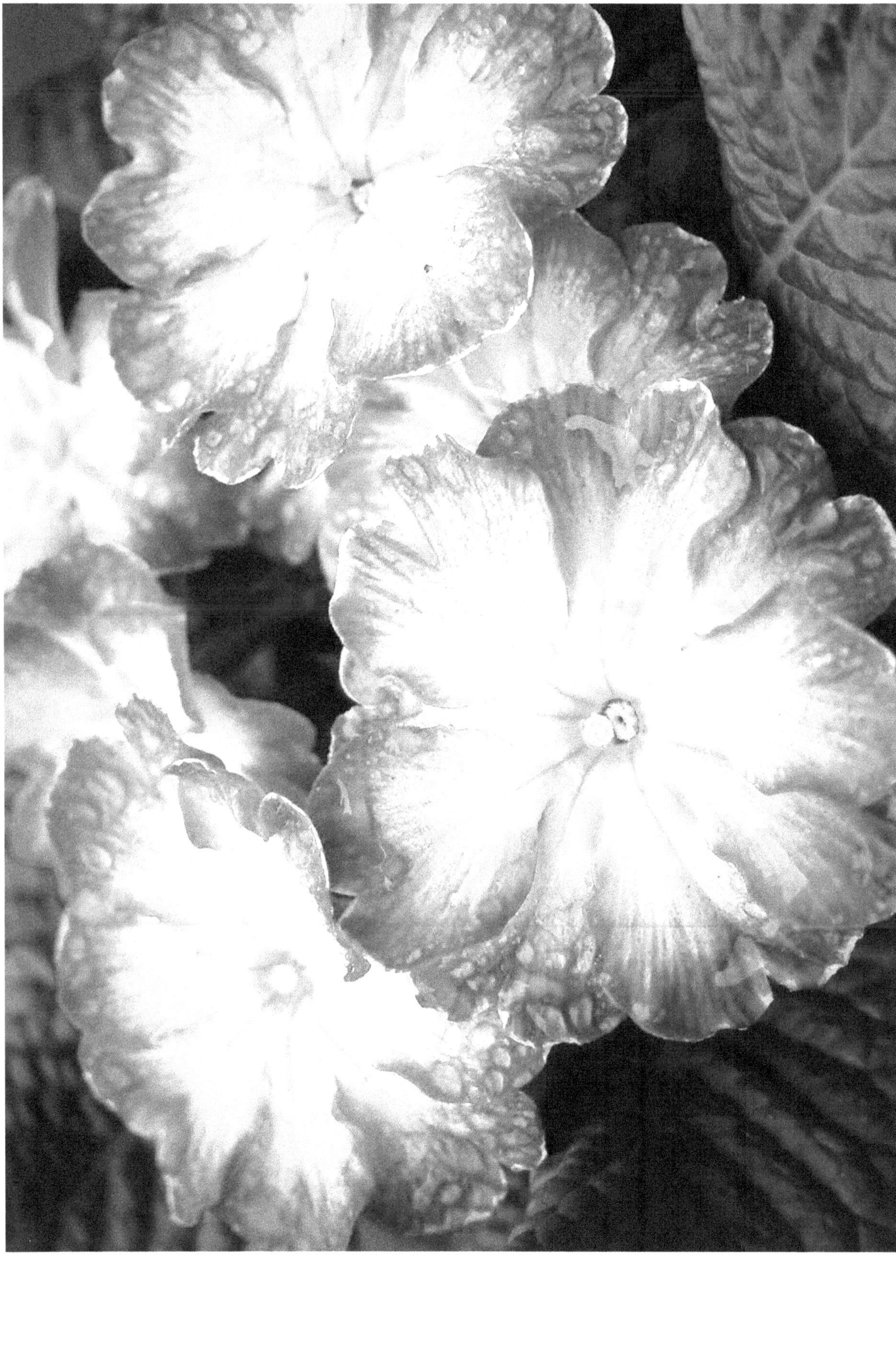

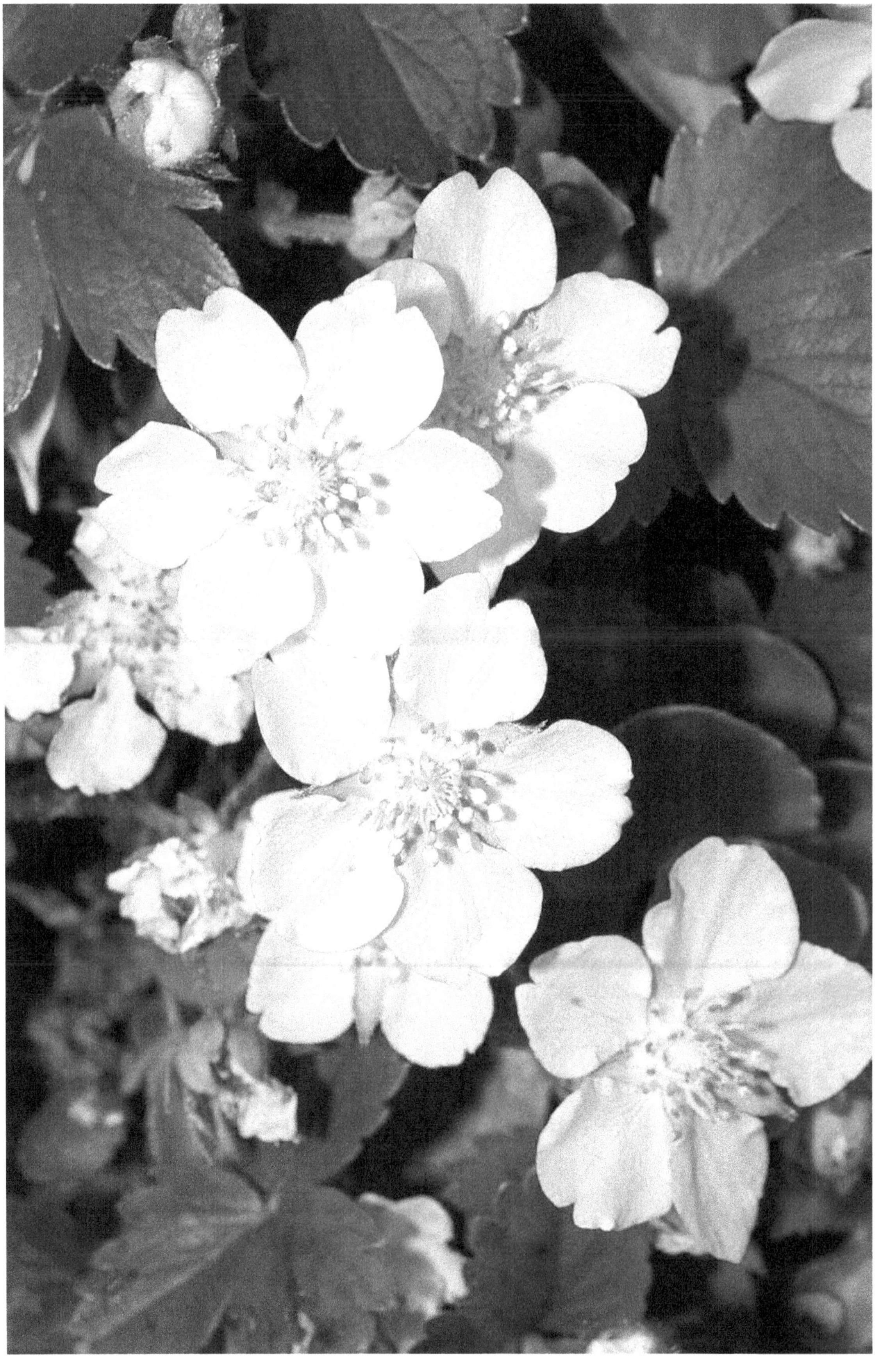

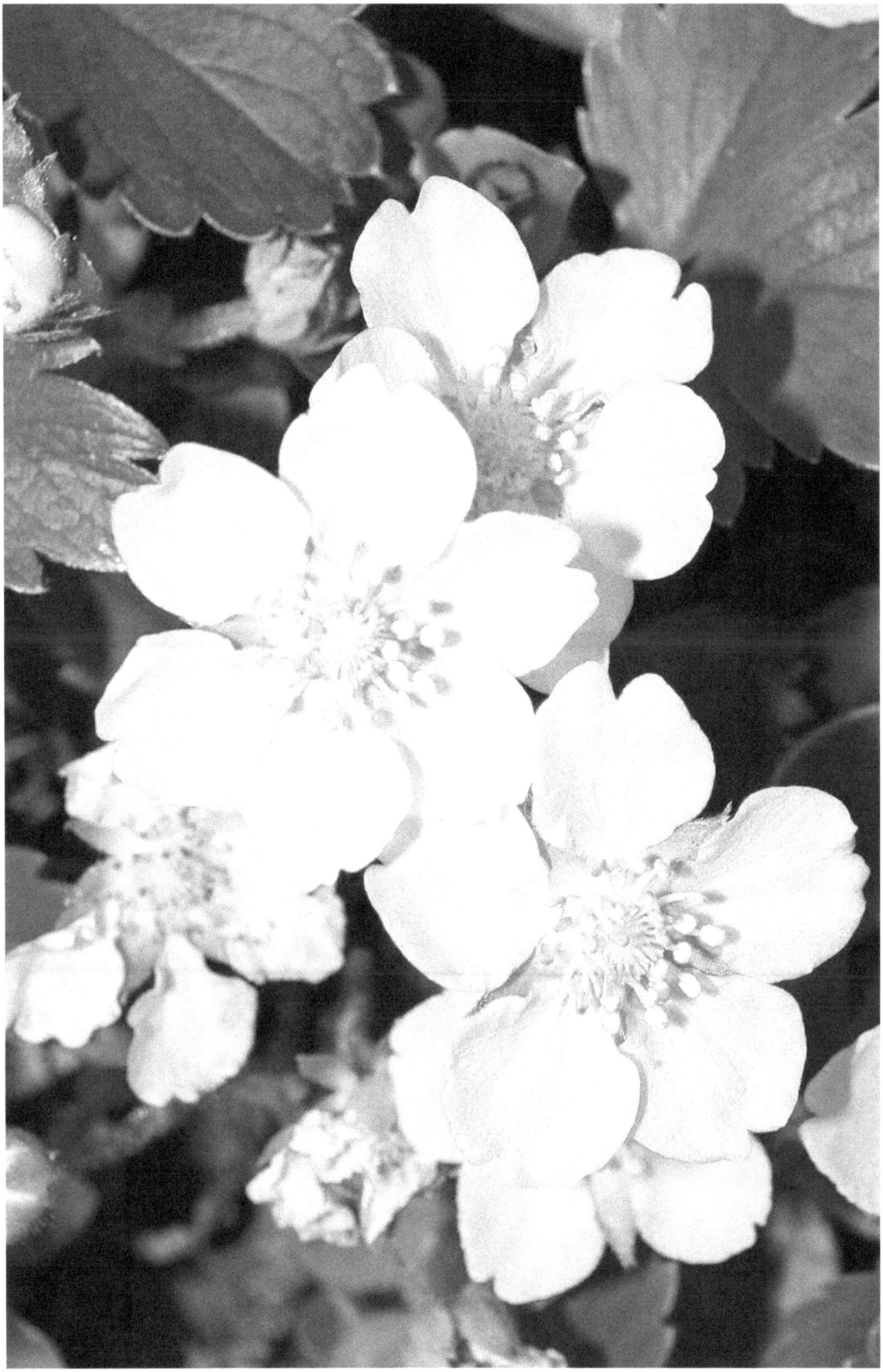

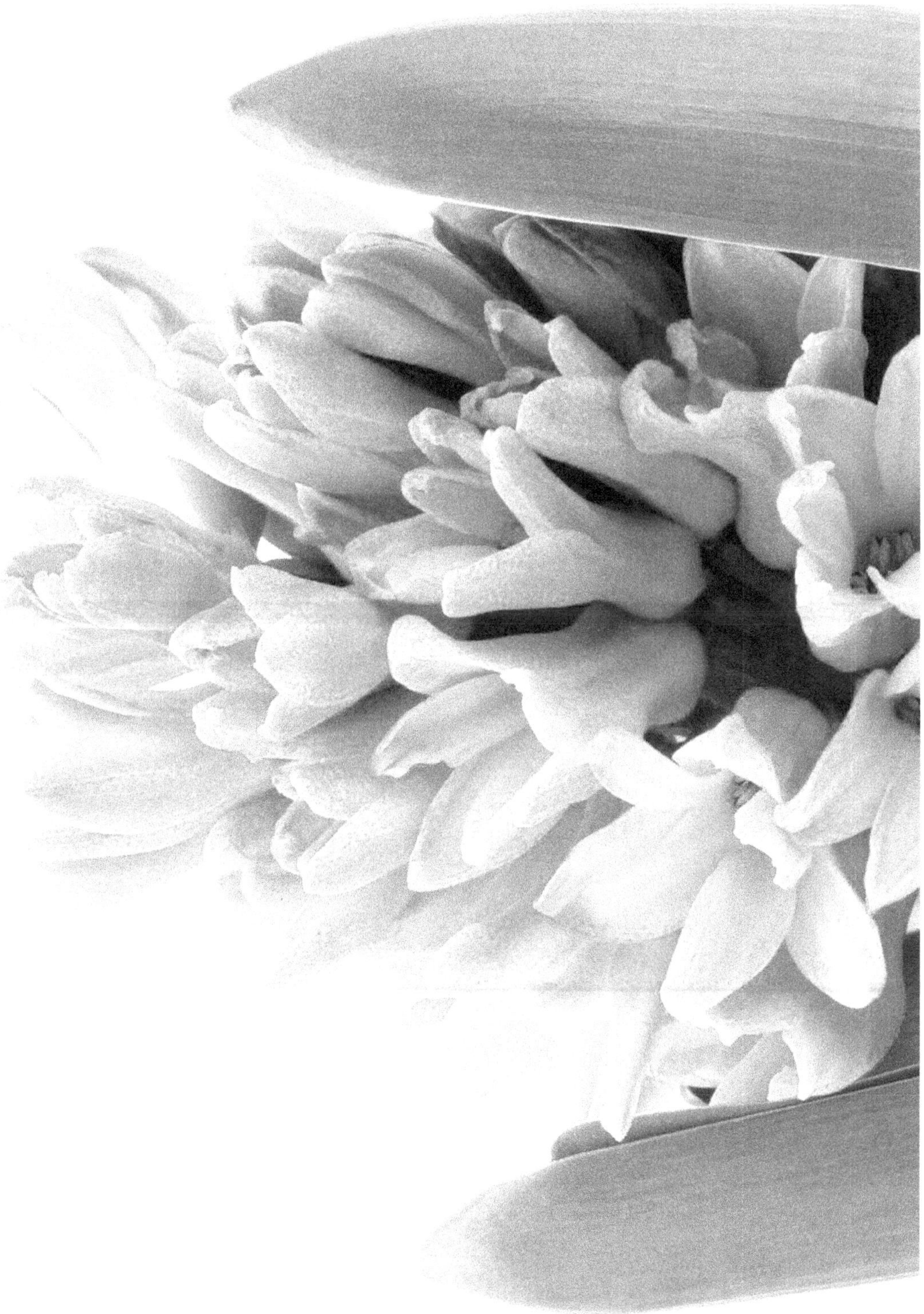

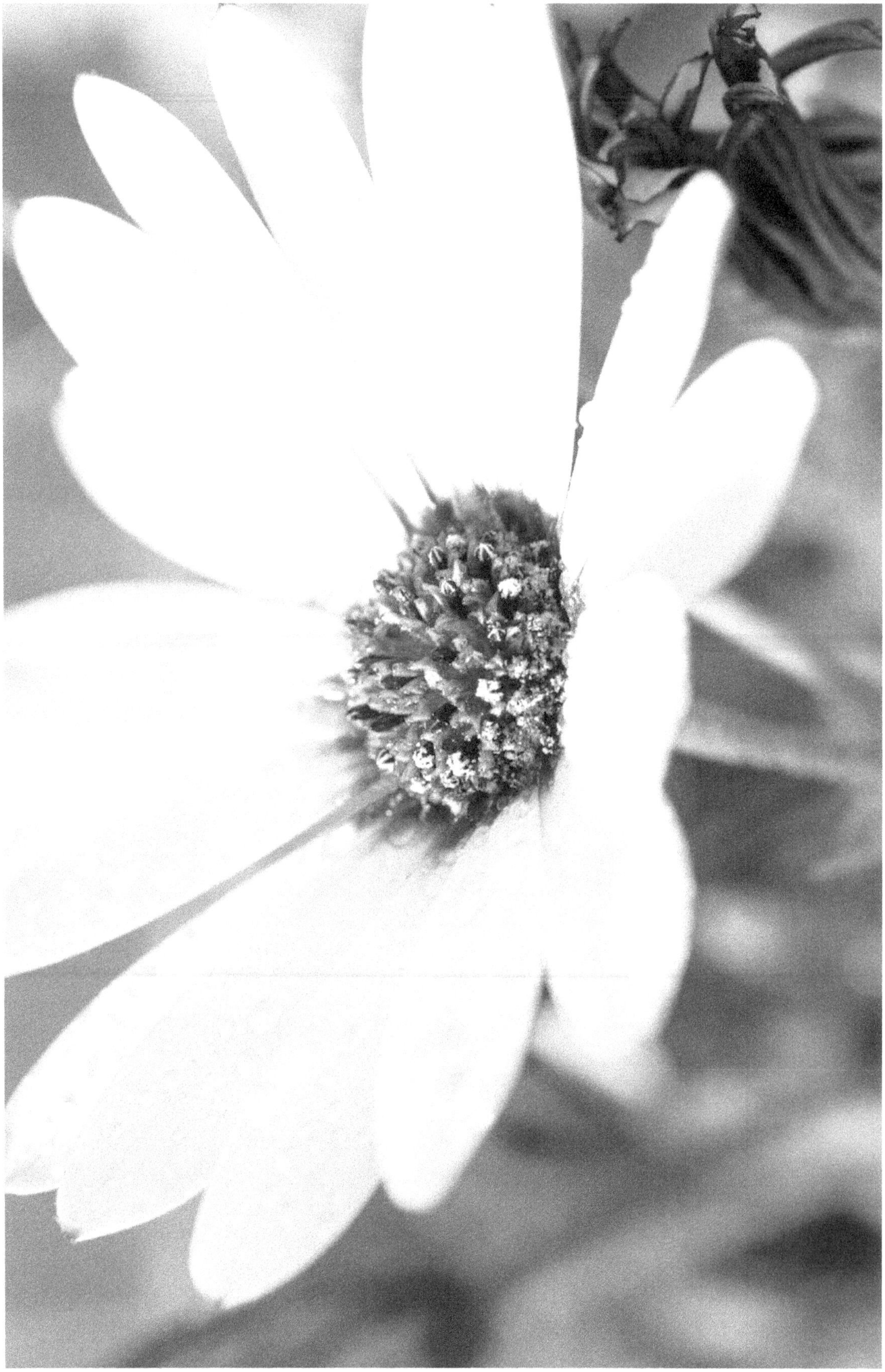

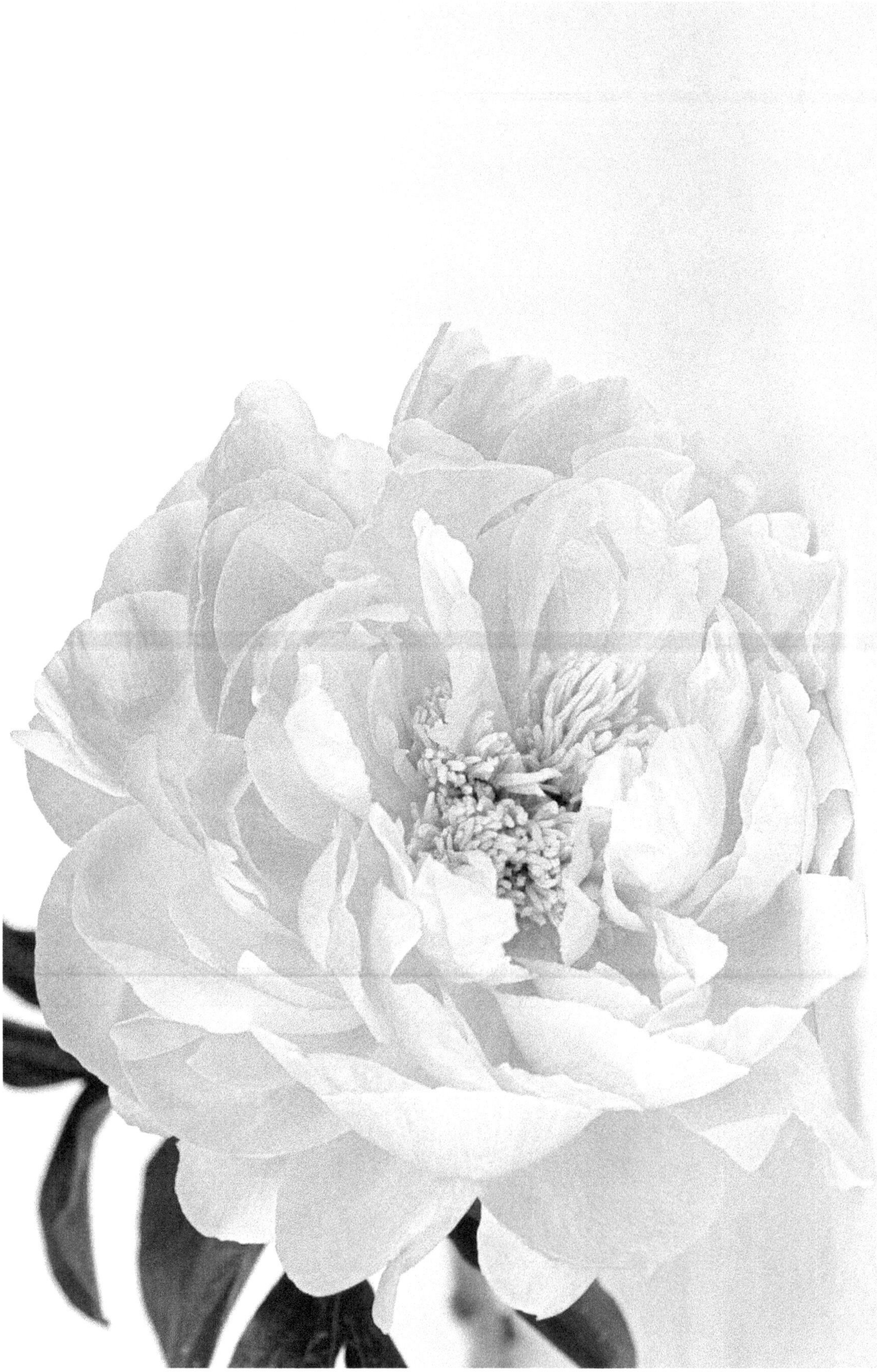

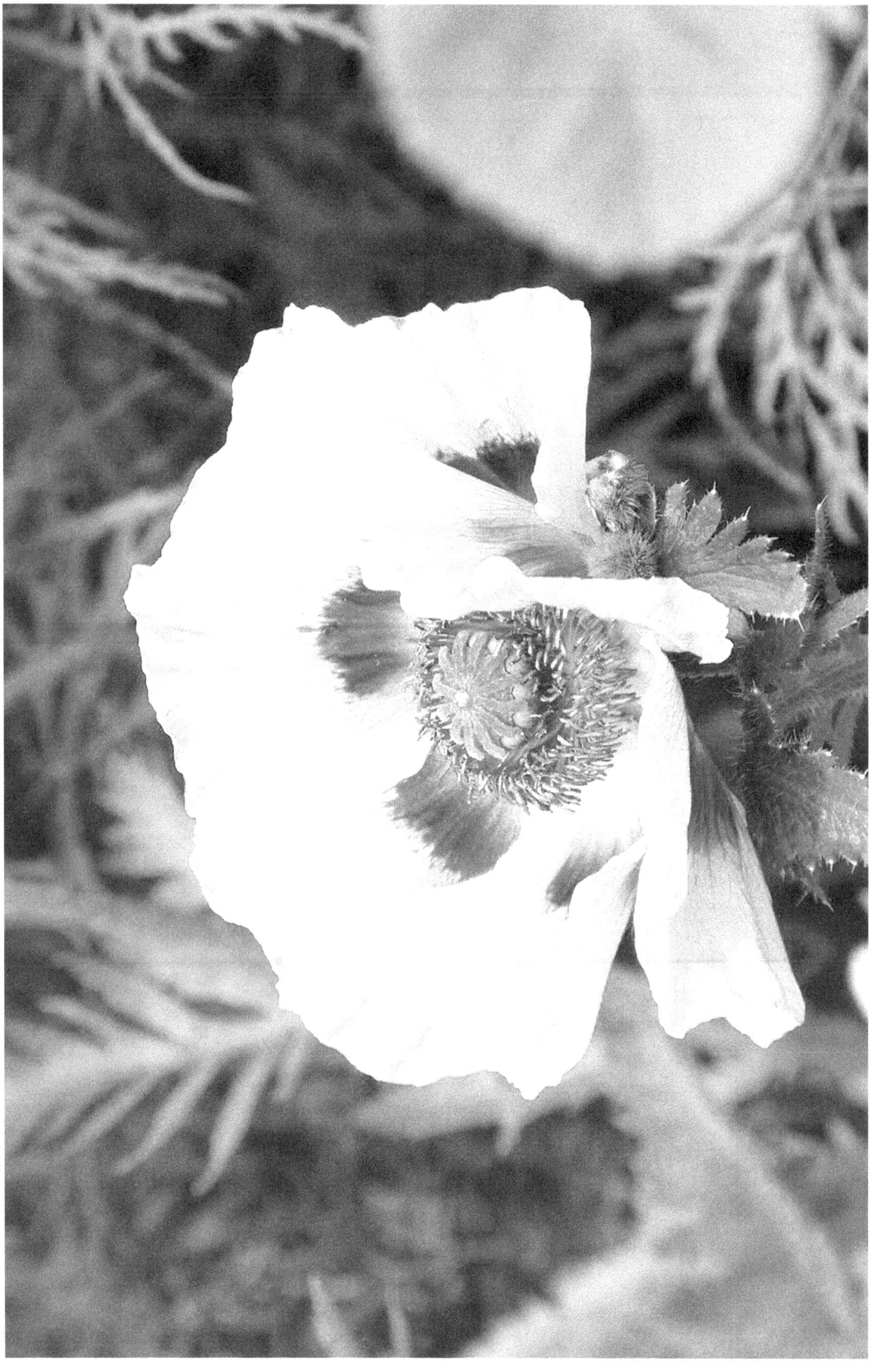

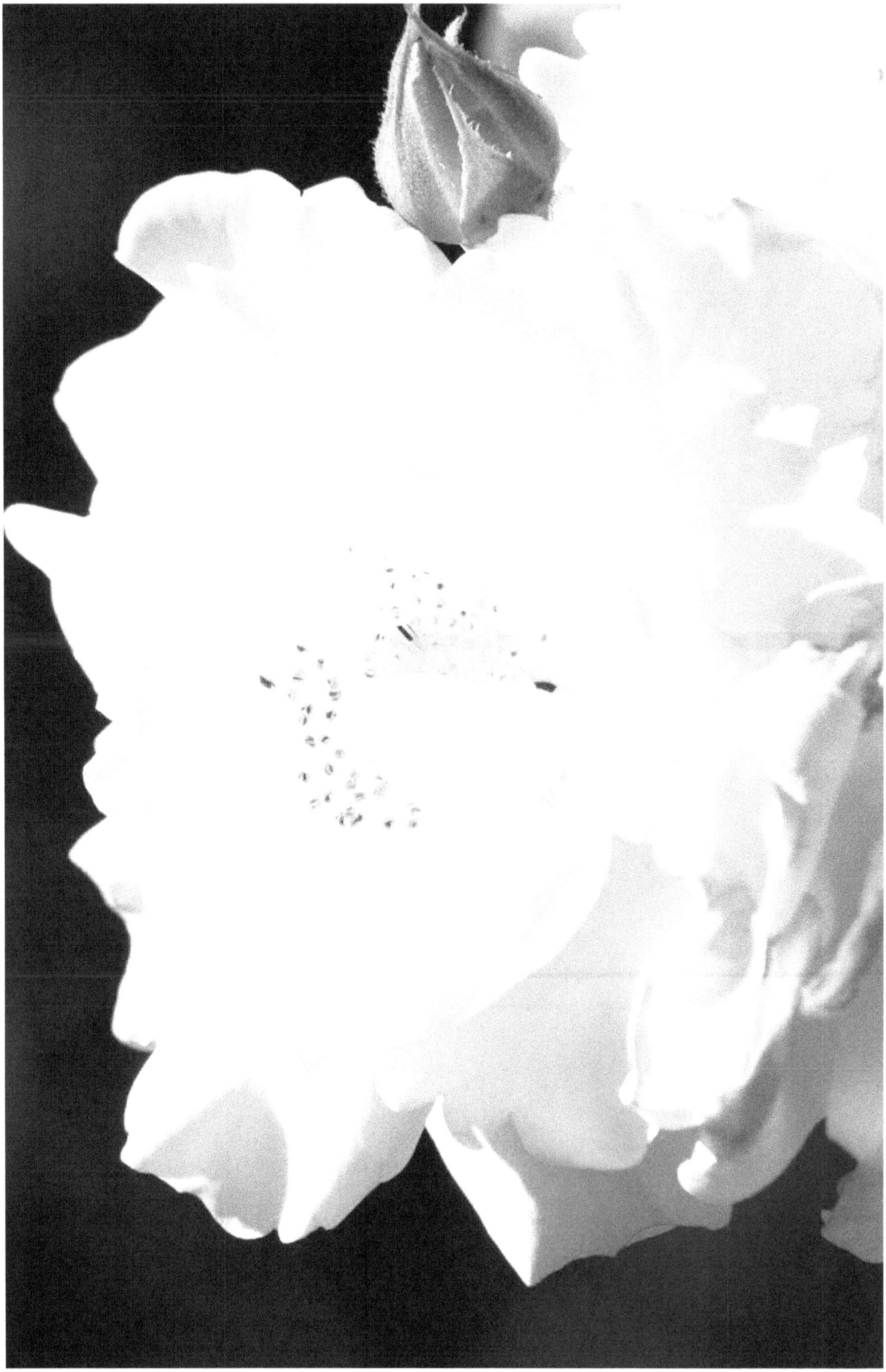

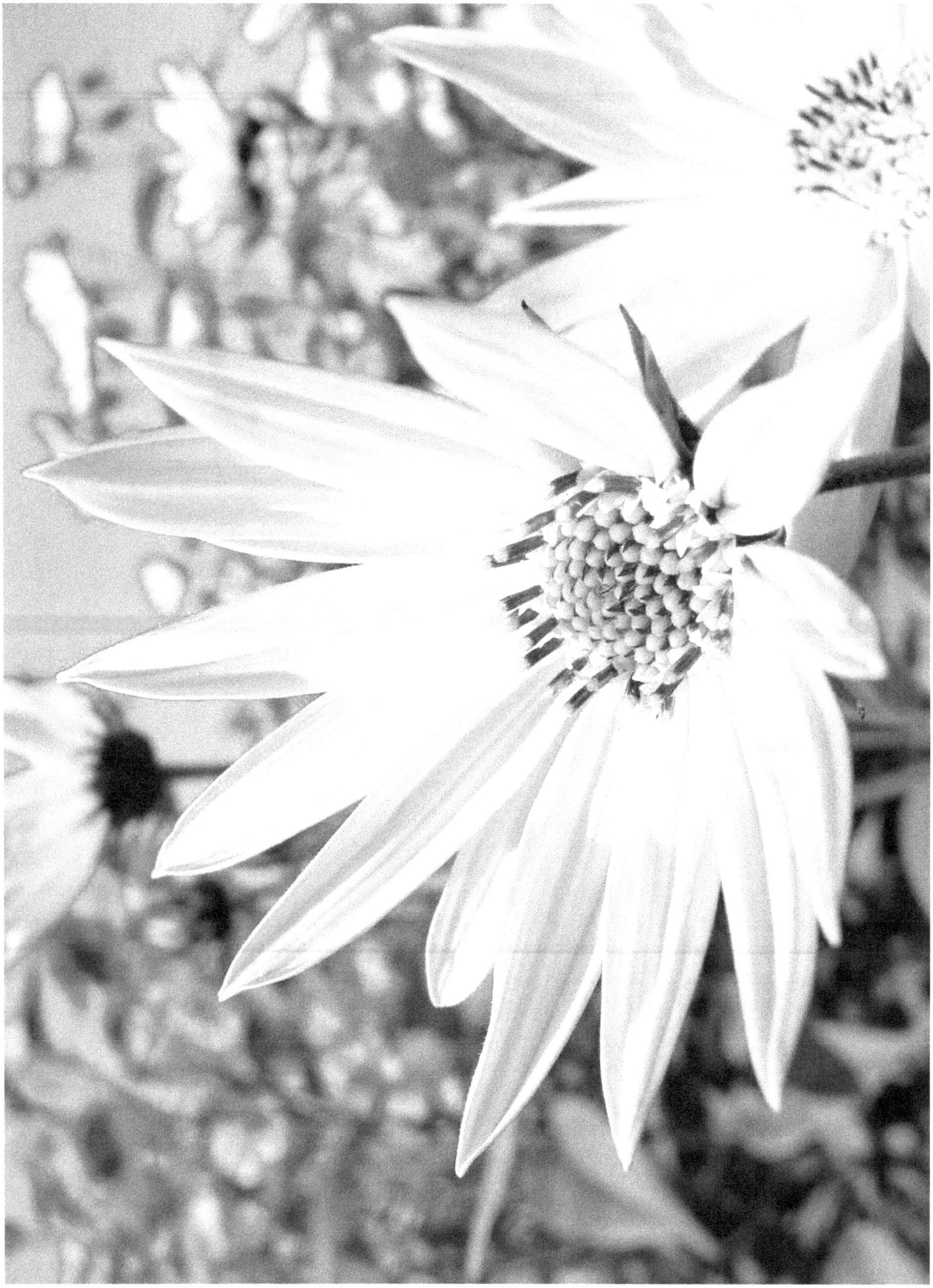

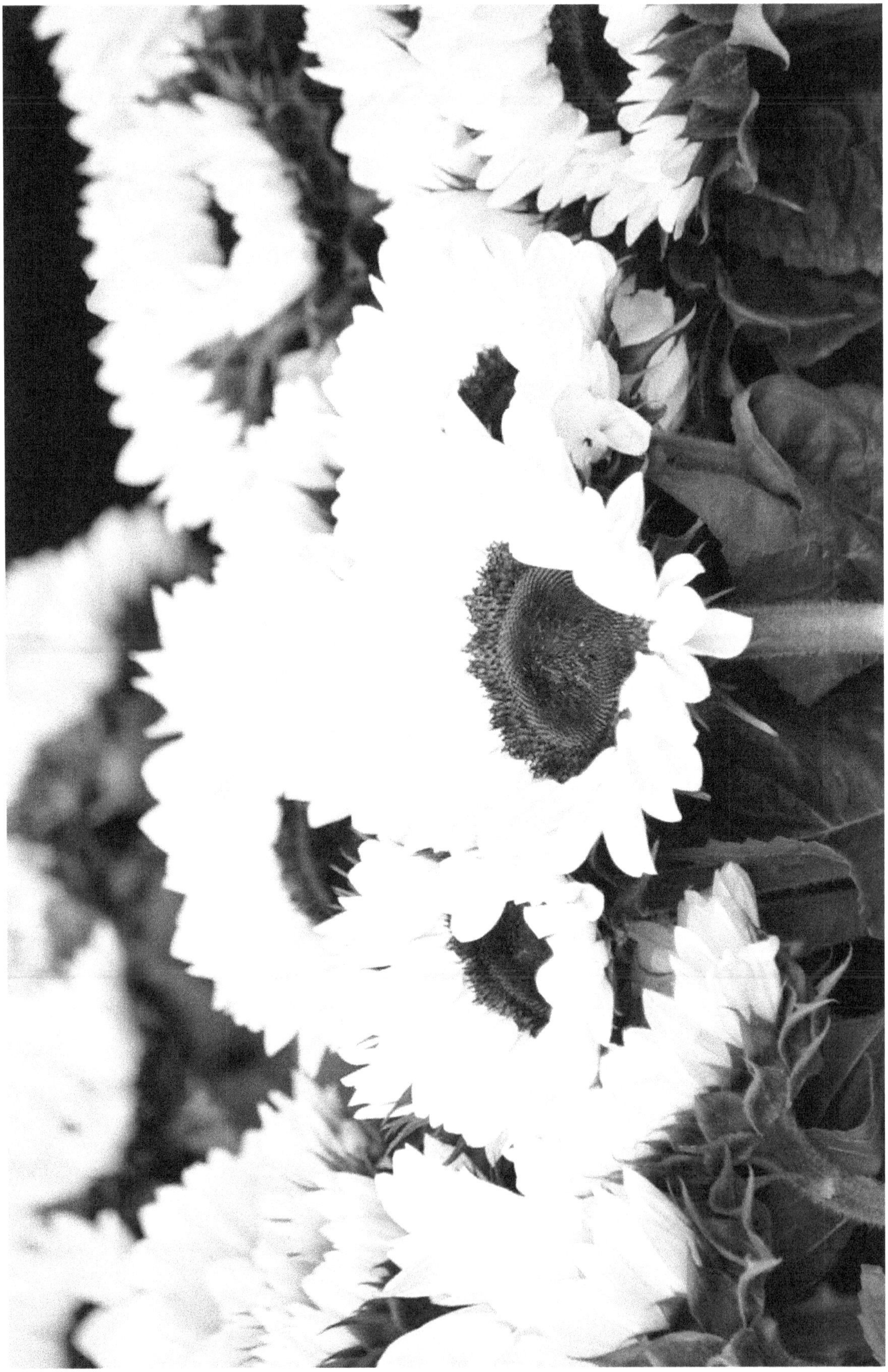

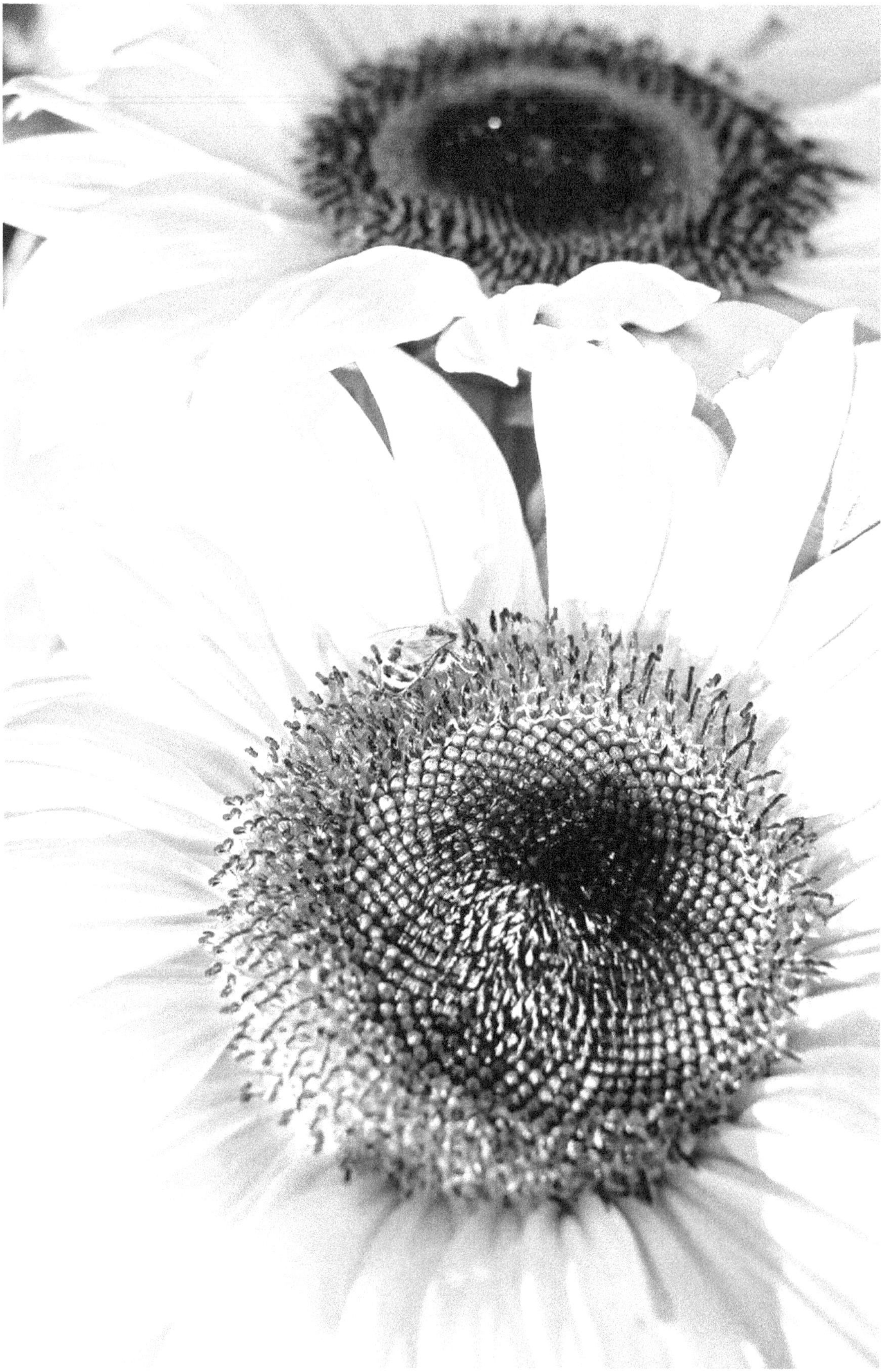

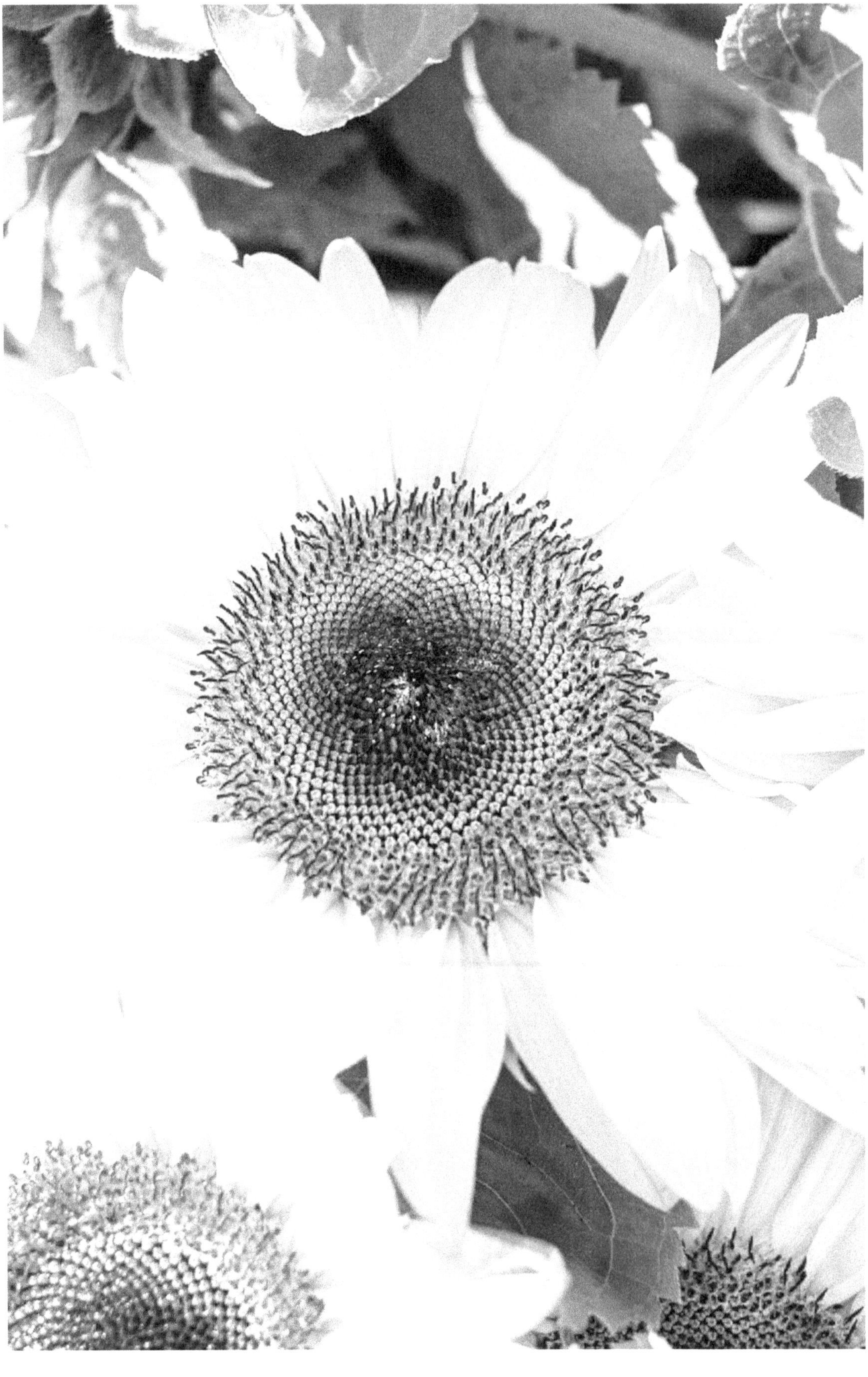

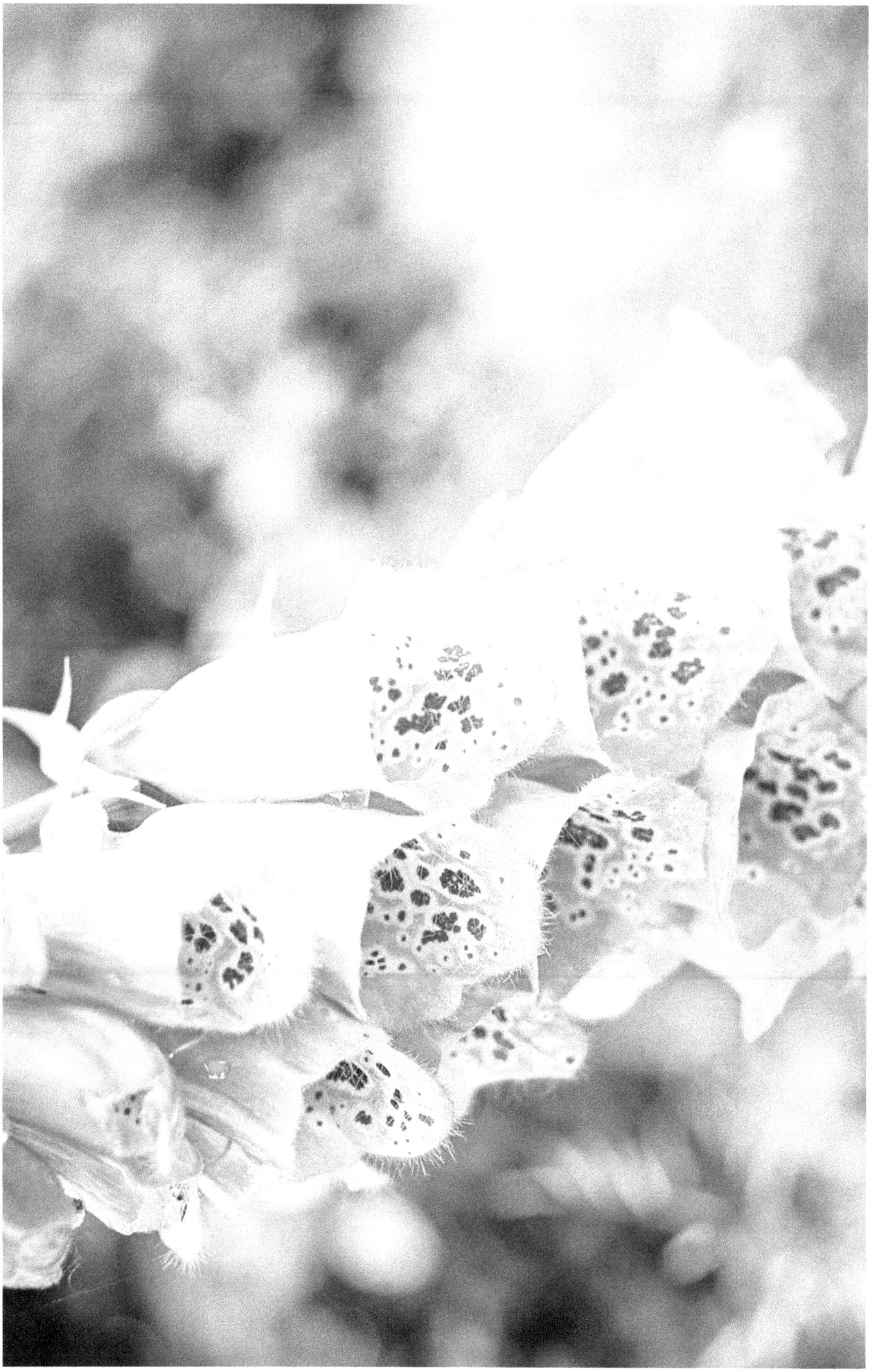

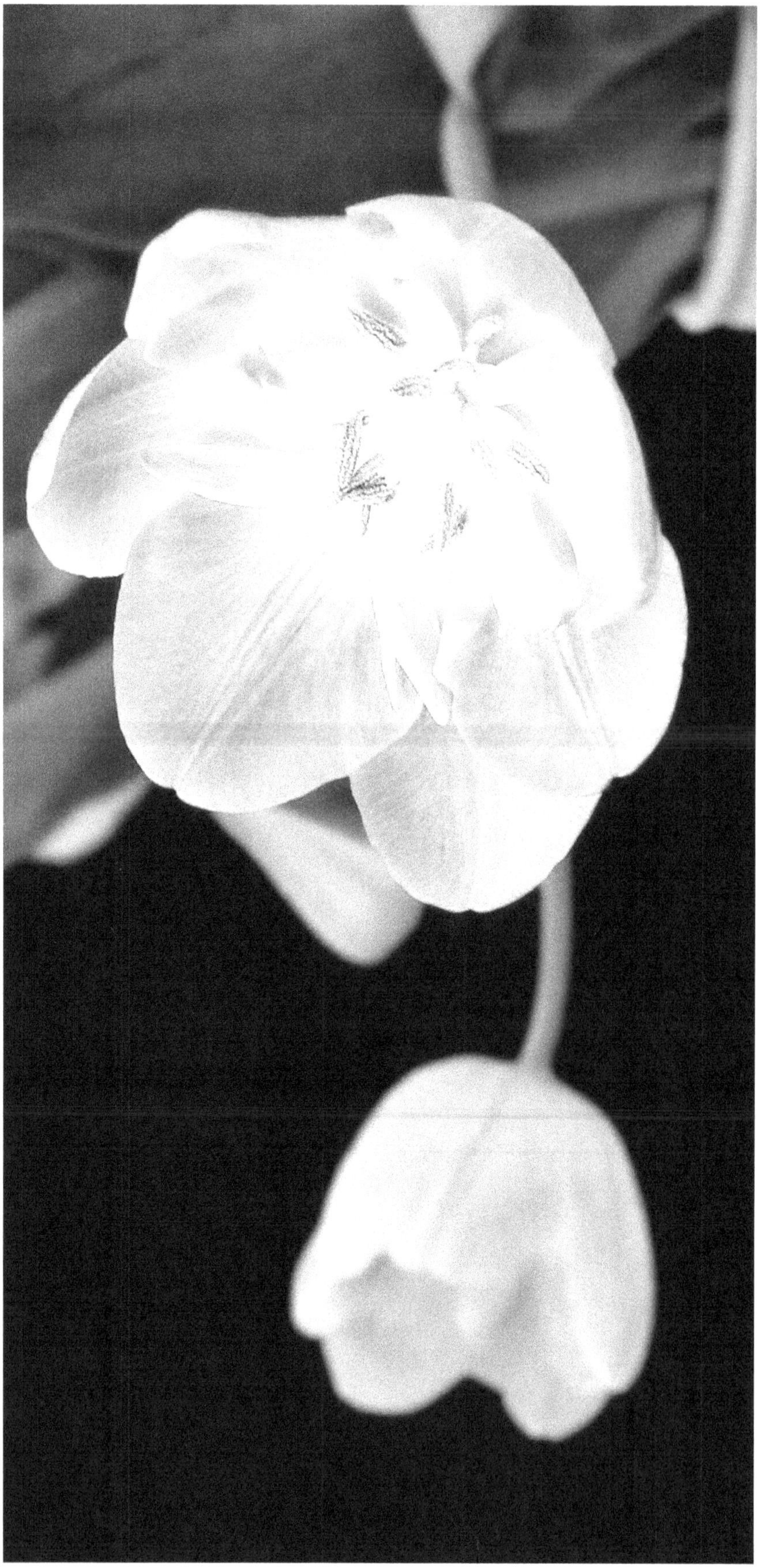

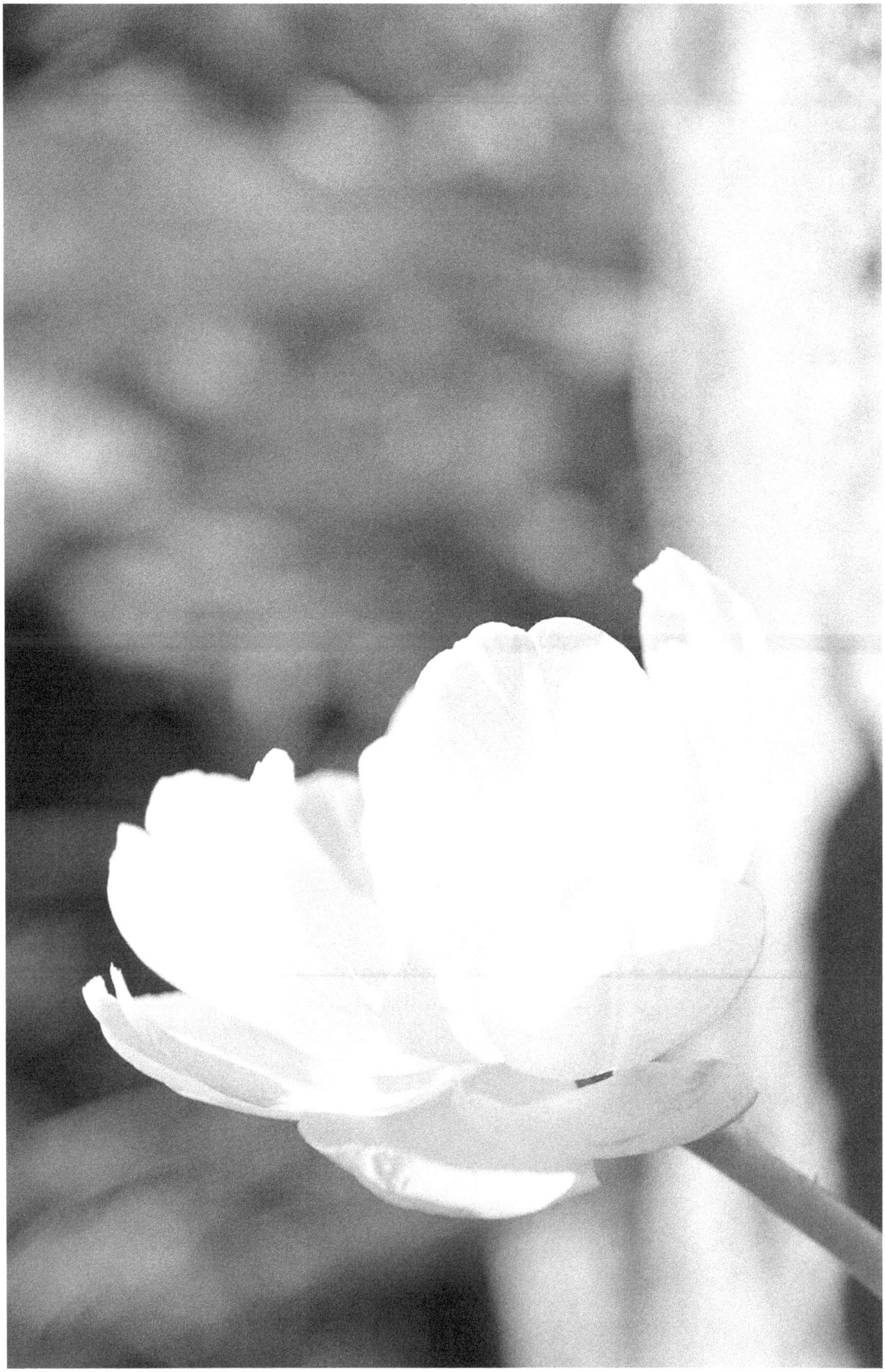

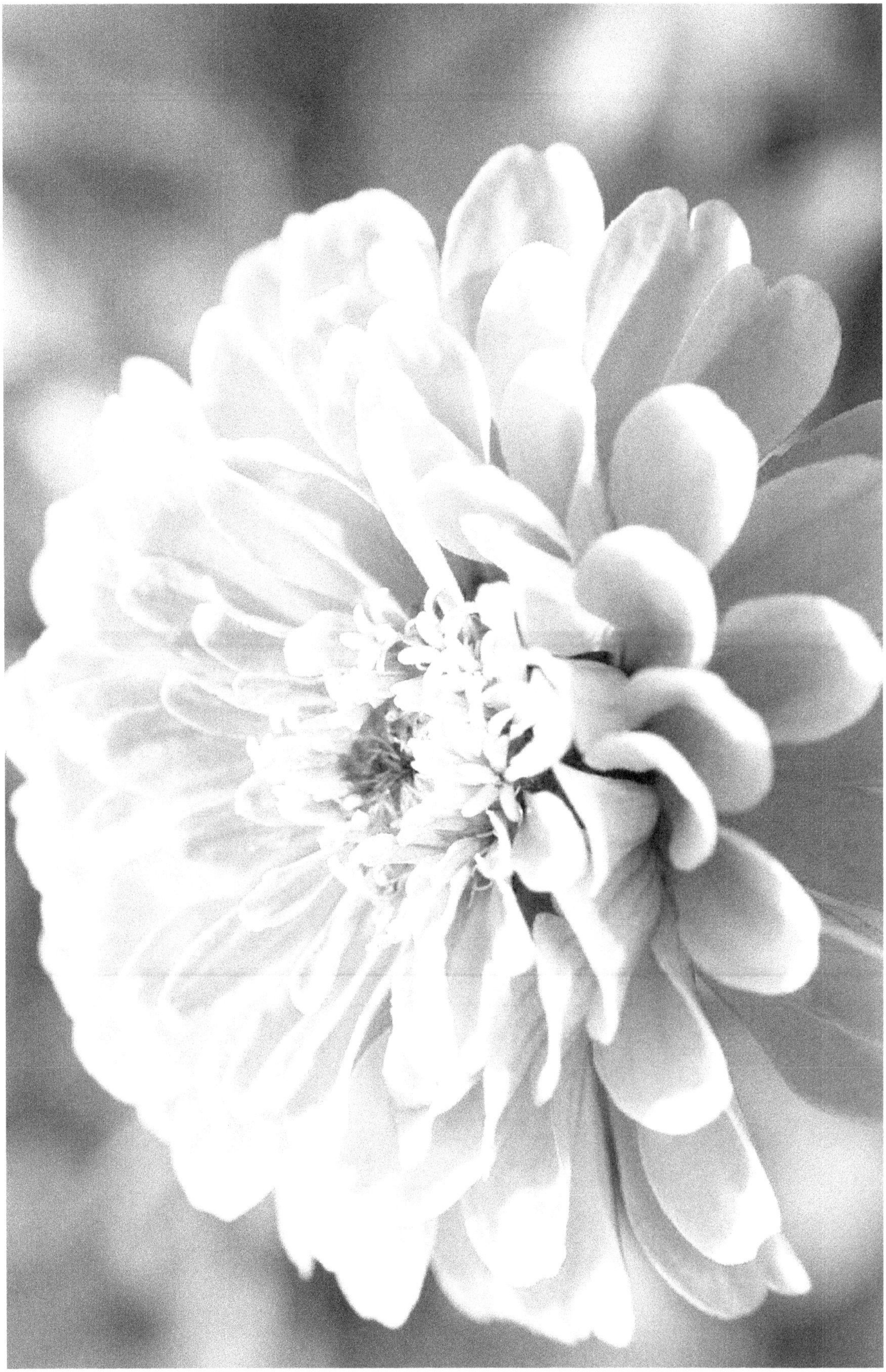

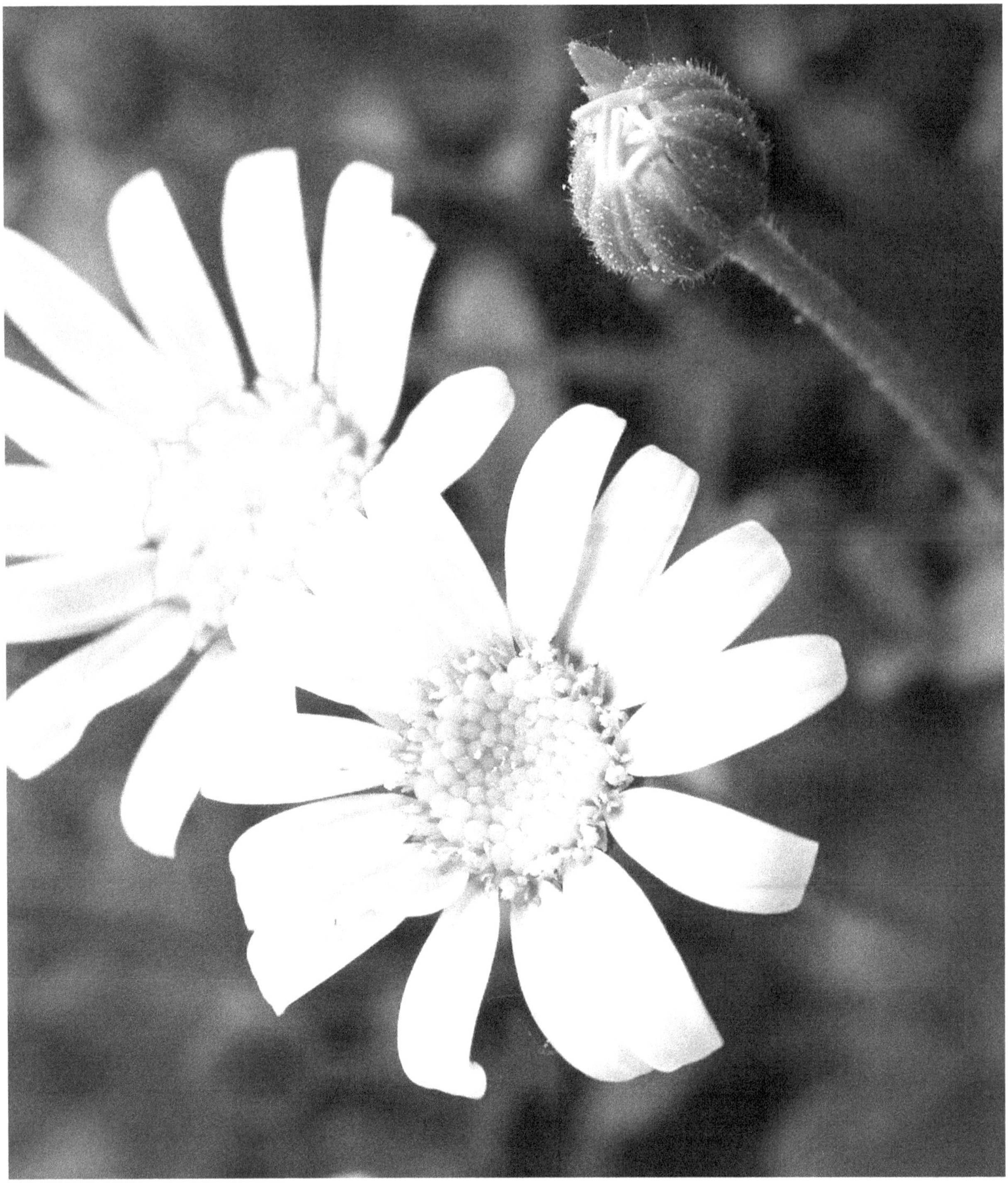

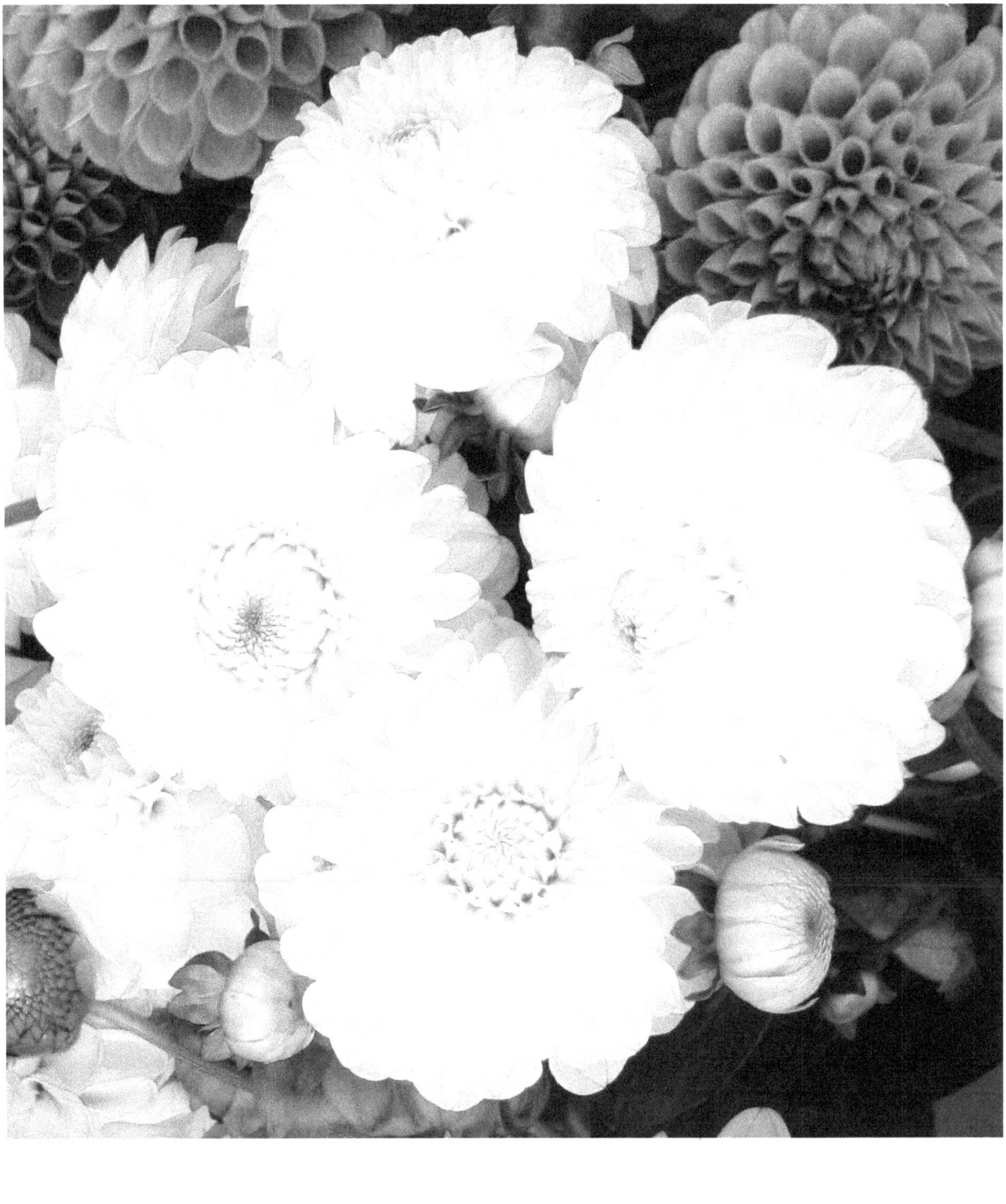

www.ingramcontent.com/pod-product-compliance
Lightning Source LLC
Chambersburg PA
CBHW080550190526
45169CB00007B/2715
* 9 7 8 1 5 3 7 0 7 7 2 7 7 *